The Economics of Energy

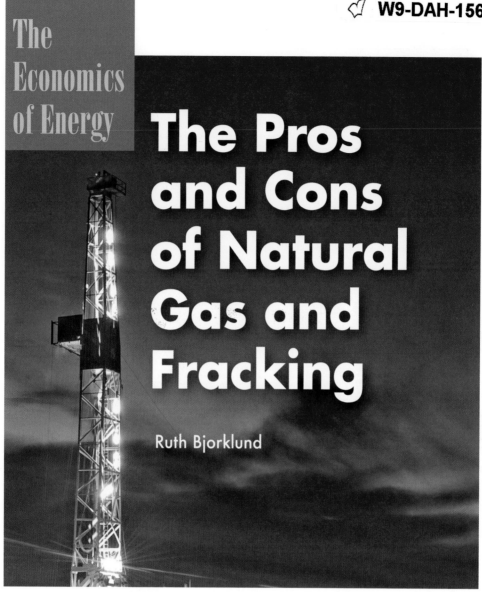

The Pros and Cons of Natural Gas and Fracking

Ruth Bjorklund

Cavendish Square

New York

Published in 2015 by Cavendish Square Publishing, LLC
243 5th Avenue, Suite 136, New York, NY 10016

Website: cavendishsq.com

This publication represents the opinions and views of the author based on his or her personal experience, knowledge, and research. The information in this book serves as a general guide only. The author and publisher have used their best efforts in preparing this book and disclaim liability rising directly or indirectly from the use and application of this book.

CPSIA Compliance Information: Batch #WS14CSQ

All websites were available and accurate when this book was sent to press.

Library of Congress Cataloging-in-Publication Data

Bjorklund, Ruth, author.
The pros and cons of natural gas and fracking / Ruth Bjorklund.
    pages cm. — (The economics of energy)
Includes bibliographical references and index.
ISBN 978-1-62712-921-3 (hardcover) ISBN 978-1-62712-923-7 (ebook)
1. Natural gas—Economic aspects—Juvenile literature. 2. Natural gas—Environmental aspects—Juvenile literature. 3. Hydraulic fracturing—Economic aspects—Juvenile literature. 4. Hydraulic fracturing—Environmental aspects—Juvenile literature. I. Title.

TP350.B56 2015
333.8'233—dc23

                    2014003270

Editorial Director: Dean Miller   Designer: Amy Greenan
Editor: Kristen Susienka   Production Manager: Jennifer Ryder-Talbot
Copy Editor: Cynthia Roby   Production Editor: David McNamara
Art Director: Jeffrey Talbot   Photo Researcher: J8 Media

Printed in the United States of America

Table of Contents

GLOBAL CARBON CYCLE

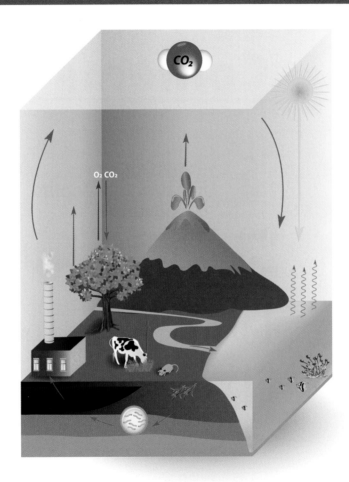

Diagram showing life cycle of carbon. Carbon made from decomposed organic matter is ingested by plants and animals. Plants absorb carbon. Animals release carbon into the atmosphere when they breathe. Carbon extracted from the earth in the form of coal, oil, and natural gas is also released into the atmosphere, either as an escaping gas or when burned for fuel.

Chapter 1

Up From the Depths

The element **carbon** is the basis of all organic (obtained from living things) molecules. Hundreds of millennia ago, the decayed remains of organisms—plants, land animals, and marine life—became embedded in the earth in carbon-filled rock formations. Some of the carbon deposits developed into coal, oil, and natural gas. These fossilized deposits can be burned for fuel, hence the name, **fossil fuels**. Fossil fuels were formed some 360 to 285 million years ago, well before dinosaurs roamed Earth.

During this period, called the Carboniferous era, Earth was covered in oceans, rivers, and swamps. Abundant vegetation and animal life thrived by soaking up water and absorbing energy from the sun. As plants and animals died, their remains sank to the bottom of the oceans, rivers, and swamps, and formed layers of a soft material called peat. Over time, crushed minerals in the form of silt and sand covered the peat and compressed it. The silt and sand hardened to form what is called **shale**, a laminated and somewhat brittle form of **sedimentary rock**. The heat created from the pressure and the sedimentary rock compressed the decayed material into a liquid chemical compound made up of carbon and hydrogen called hydrocarbon.

Fossil Fuels

The differences between the various fossil fuels are a result of the makeup of the original organic plant and animal materials, their age, and the combination of minerals, temperature, and the weight of the upper layers of rock. When burned, fossil fuels release the stored energy they had once derived from the sun.

The most abundant fossil fuel in the world is coal—a hard, black substance composed of carbon, hydrogen, oxygen, nitrogen, and sulfur. Coal was formed when layers of decomposed trees and plants were covered over by silt and seawater. The seawater contained large amounts of sulfur. Later when the seas dried up, the sulfur remained in the coal.

Oil and natural gas developed along similar lines to each other, and their deposits are often found close together. Both were created by decomposed organisms that lived in water. After the prehistoric rivers and seas receded, increased temperature, pressure, and an onslaught of bacteria combined forces to heat up the organic remains buried under layers of rock. Mostly, this process created a thick liquid, or oil. However, in deeper areas, the temperature and pressure were greater and the heating process intensified, creating what is known as natural gas. Over eons, as Earth changed, shifted, and folded, pockets were formed in the rocks that contained oil and natural gas. Some rocks have pores, or small openings, that can absorb fluids or air. In rocks that are porous, the oil and natural gas can be found inside the rock itself. In nonporous rock, the oil and natural gas cannot escape, so pools of oil and gas form beneath the rock. The heavy nonporous rock that sits on top of the oil and gas is referred to as **cap-rock**. Some deposits of oil and natural gas manage to flow up through Earth's crust and seep from the ground.

Near Baku, in present day Azerbaijan, a long wall of fire burns, fueled by natural gas seeping from below the surface. Although the region has for centuries been called the "land of fire," many such sites have gone quiet as the natural gas has been mined. But this site, called Yanar Dag, remains continuously aflame.

Oil is usually black in color, but is also sometimes green or clear. It also ranges in viscosity, or thickness. Natural gas, however, is lighter than air. It is a clear, odorless, flammable liquid made mostly of **methane**, as well as carbon dioxide, nitrogen, and hydrogen sulfide. Sometimes oil and natural gas combine underground. The result is a substance called **petroleum**, from the Latin word meaning "rock oil."

In present day Azerbaijan, the Fire Temple of Baku was an altar of sacrifice dating back to the tenth century. The temple, where many fire rituals were performed, was built above a natural gas seep.

Discovery

Between 6,000 and 2,000 years BCE, people in ancient Persia discovered and made use of natural gas seeps in what are now the countries Iran and Azerbaijan. Early Persian records suggest they first discovered the seeping gas when it was struck by lightning, which created a flame. The ancient Persians used the natural gas as fuel for "eternal flames" in religious worship. The Persian military coated their arrows

A DEEPER DIVE

Fire on the Mountain

In ancient Greece, around 1000 BCE, a goat herdsman was tending his flock on Mount Parnassus, near the town of Delphi. He came upon what appeared to be a "burning spring." Unexplainable flames rose out of a fissure—or narrow opening of considerable length and depth—in the rock. The vision astounded the herdsman and, according to legend, he fell into a frenzied state and began to foretell the future. The villagers believed the flames were divine, and word of the prophecies spread. Many visited the site to discover their own fates, but many also fell to their deaths in the fissure. It was determined that only one person, a priestess, would sit by the fire and offer prophecies inspired by the flame. She became known as the Oracle of Delphi. Of course, the flame was a result of a lightning strike on a natural gas seep.

In 1866, Charles Léo Lesquereux determined that bitumen, or petroleum, was formed from marine algae.

in oil, set them on fire, and then shot them at their enemies. Other ancient societies, such as the Greeks, Sumerians, Assyrians, and Babylonians, also witnessed sudden eruptions of flame when lightning struck seeping natural gas.

It is believed that the Chinese were the first to use natural gas as a fuel source in 1000 BCE. They placed bamboo stalks into the ground to extract natural gas that lay just below the surface. They used the gas to heat seawater and extract its salt. They also made lanterns by collecting the gas in leather bags and lighting the gas that escaped through a small slit on fire. Around 340 CE, the Chinese attached metal drill bits to bamboo poles to mine for oil.

In ancient times, the mixture of natural gas and oil was called bitumen. Philosophers debated whether bitumen was organic or inorganic. The ancient Greek philosopher Aristotle believed that bitumen was formed from a stone made of sulfur from deep within Earth. During the Renaissance period in Europe (fourteenth to seventeenth centuries), the German scientist Agricola also proposed that bitumen was made from "exhalations" of sulfur from deep inside Earth. Several years later, another German scientist suggested that bitumen came from the sap of ancient trees. In 1866, Charles Léo Lesquereux determined that bitumen, or petroleum, was formed from marine algae. In 1907, two American **geologists** concluded that petroleum deposits found in California were formed by single-cell aquatic organisms called "diatoms."

A DEEPER DIVE

Father of American Paleobotany

In the 1830s, the mother of Swiss scientist Charles Léo Lesquereux hoped that her son would become a priest. Instead, the young man devoted himself to natural science, specifically, the study of mosses and peat. Lesquereux was commissioned by governments throughout Europe to study and describe peat bogs. In 1848, he came to America to teach and study. He eventually settled in Columbus, Ohio, where he used his extensive knowledge of peat to examine the origins of coal formations in the region. Lesquereux was the author of more than fifty scholarly works on bryology (study of mosses) and paleobotany (study of ancient plants), including the official U.S. Geological Survey studies for Ohio, Pennsylvania, Illinois, Kentucky, Arkansas, and West Virginia. His understanding of ancient plants and rock formations led to more modern and efficient means of discovering and extracting fossil fuels. In 1864, he was one of the first scientists elected to the National Academy of Science.

New Energy

More than 500 thousand years ago, humans learned to depend on fire for cooking, warmth, lighting, and energy. Documents from the Middle East indicate that beginning in the ninth century, chemists had learned to distill petroleum, and use the fuel for lamps. In the thirteenth century, Italian explorer Marco Polo described Persians in Baku, a city in present-day Azerbaijan, collecting oil from large shallow seeps. In the sixteenth century, Great Britain was running out of wood and had exhausted many of its peat bogs. The country then turned to coal as a fuel for powering machinery and mills. This was the start of the Industrial Revolution, when Europe and later the United States were transformed from agrarian societies into urban industrial societies.

In seventeenth-century America, French explorers observed Native Americans living near Lake Erie igniting natural gas seeps to make fire for cooking and warmth. They also used the gas to make medicine. In 1821, a man named William Hart noticed gas bubbling from a creek. He dug a 27-foot- (8.2-meter-) deep hole and hit shale. From there, he drilled a hole through the shale rock and 70 feet (21.3 m) down discovered a pocket of natural gas. He used hollow logs as pipes to move the gas into his home. Later he was able to power a few shops, businesses, and street lamps in the town of Fredonia, New York. Taking advantage of Hart's discovery, some businessmen formed the first natural gas company in the United States: the Fredonia Natural Gas Company.

In 1859, a railroad engineer named Colonel Edwin Drake drilled one of the first oil and natural gas wells near Lake Erie. He piped the liquid fuel 5.5 miles (8.85 kilometers) to Titusville, Pennsylvania. His work demonstrated that extracting and delivering oil and gas could be done safely and with relatively few difficulties. Oil prospectors in Pennsylvania, New York, Kentucky, and West Virginia took heed. In searching for drilling sites, they often used nitroglycerin, an explosive, to crack the rock to look for oil. Although highly dangerous, the first fracturing methods were successful.

In the United States during the nineteenth century, natural gas was mostly used for lighting. In 1891, one of the first pipelines to carry the gas was built. It was 120 miles (193 km) long, but it was expensive and not very well made. By the end of the century, gas lights had been replaced by electric lights, and natural gas was no longer viewed as an important source of fuel.

Most of the natural gas that had been used to this point was actually derived by processing coal. There were few natural gas wells and little infrastructure to transport it. Natural gas found in the ground alongside coal or oil was usually left behind to vaporize or be burnt off. After World War II, however, new technologies in metalworking and pipeline construction helped extend the infrastructure needed to effectively transport oil and natural gas. In the 1960s, thousands of miles of natural gas pipelines were built, and new uses for the fuel developed in manufacturing, heating, and operating household appliances.

A Delicate Balance

Since the nineteenth century, countries around the world have actively mined for fossil fuels. Techniques and methods have improved, creating cleaner, safer drilling sites and more efficient means of delivering the fuels to market. However, there are many shifts occurring in today's

A DEEPER DIVE

Lab Discovery

In 1843, a German scientist named Robert Bunsen lost his right eye in an explosion in his laboratory. He had been studying organic chemistry, but with his now-reduced vision he turned to the study of inorganic chemicals and elements. His work entailed identifying elements and the physical composition of molecules through the use of light and heat. His method was to super-heat a material to a specific temperature and study the color, or spectra, of the light the material emitted. The fuel, burned in laboratory burners, emitted smoke in large quantities, contaminating some test results. The color of the burner's flame mixed with the subject material's color, and thus tainted Bunsen's experiments. Bunsen then made improvements on a burner once developed by scientist Michael Faraday. Bunsen used natural gas and mixed it with air to light his laboratory burner. The flame burned steady and colorless. It could burn at very high temperatures, but could easily be regulated by adjusting the ratio of air to gas. The natural gas burned clean—combustion was virtually 100 percent complete, no matter the temperature. The success of the Bunsen burner demonstrated that natural gas was a clean and efficient fuel.

German scientist Robert Bunsen used his invention of a laboratory burner to conclude that each element emits light in its own distinct wavelength.

energy outlook. Coming to the forefront is a new technology to extract natural gas and oil called **hydraulic fracturing,** more commonly known as fracking.

The need for oil and natural gas and the methods used to acquire fossil fuels are of significant concern to the United States and the rest of the world. The global population is expected to rise to about nine billion people by the year 2040, and a plentiful supply of affordable energy will be needed. All energy production, especially mining for fossil fuels, must be balanced by taking into account many criteria, such as cost, employment, climate change, environmental protection, and safety. As Alex Prud'homme, author of *Hydrofracking: What Everyone Needs to Know*, explains, "Fracking is neither all good nor all bad." The debate as to whether fracking should continue or should cease is complicated and often emotional.

Oil and Natural Gas Timeline

1000–500 BCE The Chinese use bamboo pipes to collect natural gas

340 CE Chinese mine for oil in wells 800 feet (244 m) deep using metal drill bits attached to bamboo poles

1264 Italian explorer Marco Polo witnesses Persians mining seep oil

1626 French explorers witness Native Americans near Lake Erie using natural gas seeps to prepare medications

1735 French mine oil from oil sands in Alsace, France

1821 William Hart digs the first natural gas well near Fredonia, New York; the gas was eventually piped in hollow logs to fuel street lamps in Fredonia

1848 First modern oil well dug by a Russian engineer near Baku, Iran

1849 First distillation of kerosene from oil signals the end of the use of whale oil for lighting

1859 Colonel Edwin Drake completes the first oil well, and pipes oil and natural gas 5.5 miles (8.9 km) to Titusville, Pennsylvania

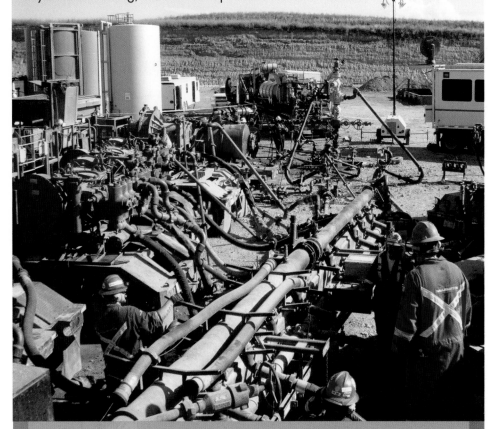

Much of the nation's natural gas production is achieved by hydraulic fracking, such as this operation in North Dakota.

1860s Prospectors in Pennsylvania, New York, West Virginia, Kentucky, and West Virginia use nitroglycerin to fracture rock in search for oil

1885 Robert Bunsen invents the Bunsen burner, the first device to burn natural gas and air to achieve a safe and controlled method for heating and cooking

1890 Manufacturers begin selling household appliances fueled by natural gas

1914–1918 Military forces at the onset of World War I plan to use horses for transportation. By war's end (1918), Great Britain boasts 56,000 trucks and 36,000 cars. The United States shipped more than 50,000 vehicles and 15,000 planes to Europe, all powered by refined petroleum

1923 Twenty-three million cars travel American roads using gasoline made from refined petroleum

1930–1950 Vast "supergiant" oil fields are discovered in Mexico, Venezuela, Russia, and several Middle Eastern countries

1948 Halliburton Company of Texas performs first hydraulic fracturing procedures in shallow wells using minimal amounts of fluid

1960 The number of U.S. domestic natural gas customers exceeds 30 million

1973 Egypt and Syria attack Israel. The United States supplies weapons to Israel—several Middle Eastern countries retaliate by placing an embargo on exports of oil to the United States. Prices of oil and gas skyrocket

1973–Present The federal government, beginning with President Gerald Ford, assures ongoing support for "energy independence" programs to develop and sustain power production using domestic fossil fuel resources, nuclear power, and renewable energy sources

1976 Federal Energy Research and Development Administration establishes the Eastern Gas Shales Project to investigate drilling and fracturing methods

1989 Oryx Engineering develops the horizontal drill that substantially increases oil and gas extraction production

1998 Engineer Nick Steinsberger of Mitchell Energy develops a technique called "slickwater fracking," a hydraulic fracturing fluid mixture that dissolves shale to release oil and gas

2002 First high-volume combined hydraulic fracturing and horizontal drilling procedures performed

2012 United States becomes the largest producer of natural gas in the world

2013 United States produces 7.3 million barrels of oil per day, a substantial increase to past production, credited in large part to hydraulic fracturing

A DEEPER DIVE

Measuring Fossil Fuels

The first commercial oil wells were developed in western Pennsylvania during the 1860s. At the time, the unexpected intensity of the flowing oil left workers searching everywhere for containers—farmhouses, barns, town dumps, hardware stores, cellars—taking any kind of barrel they could, including those made for whiskey, cider, beer, molasses, fish, and pickles. Eventually, coopers, or barrel makers, constructed barrels specifically for oil and established a standard size: 42 gallons (159 liters). To this day, oil is measured in 42-gallon (159-liter) barrels. In 2013, the United States produced 7.3 million barrels of oil per day, or 306,600,000 gallons (1.2 billion L).

Natural gas is measured by volume in cubic feet (cu ft.). It is also measured in terms of energy—the standard used is the British thermal unit (Btu). One Btu is the amount of natural gas that will produce enough energy to heat one pound of water by one degree at thermal pressure. One cubic foot (28 L) of natural gas contains about 1,027 Btus.

CRITICAL THINKING

- As the U.S. is now the largest producer of natural gas in the world, in large part because of advances in fracking technology, do you think the nation should export natural gas to other parts of the world or keep it for domestic use? Why?

- As the U.S. is able to produce more fossil fuel energy, natural gas, and oil by means of fracking, do you think it will have an important effect on world politics? What will the effect be, and what will it mean for the future of energy?

THE PATH OF FRACKING

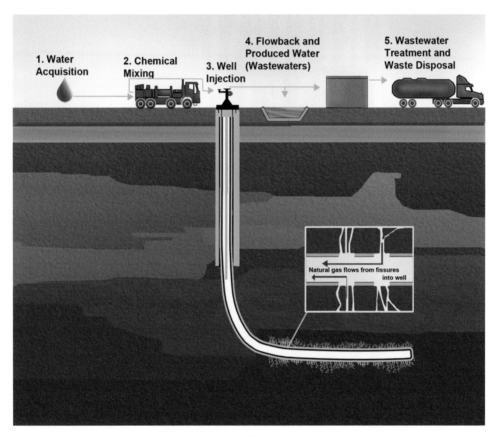

This diagram shows the basic process of fracking: water is delivered to site, mixed with slurry, and injected into a well that is drilled both vertically and horizontally, freeing the oil and natural gas. Once the water and slurry have been used, it is trucked away to wastewater treatment plants, **impoundment ponds**, **injection wells**, or to be used in other repurposed actions.

Chapter 2

Fracking: A Powerful Solution

Around the world, people have grown accustomed to using fossil fuels for nearly all their energy needs. But fossil fuels are a finite (limited) resource, meaning one day their availability will run out and they will no longer exist. There are strong movements to use other energy sources: nuclear power and renewable energies. Nuclear power is electric or motive (as a locomotive or a motor) power generated by a nuclear reactor. Renewable energies come from resources that are continually replenished, such as wind, water, solar, ocean, and geothermal power. Before the world is able to convert to other alternative fuel sources, however, people will be relying on fossil fuels for energy. Of all the fossil fuels, much attention today is placed on the rise of natural gas as a "bridge fuel" to fill the gap while the world shifts to alternative sources of energy. Natural gas, in the United States, is considered a cleaner fuel. And while it is in abundant supply, it has never been readily accessible. Now, however, due to hydraulic fracturing, natural gas and other fossil fuels can be extracted in greater quantities than ever before. Hydraulic fracturing has become the most efficient and profitable means to extract hard-to-reach natural gas and oil deposits.

Hydraulic fracturing, or fracking, is the forcing of liquid—water along with several chemicals such as hydrochloric acid, sodium chloride, methanol, and isopropyl alcohol—underground at pressure great enough to crack open shale rock and release trapped natural gas and oil. Oil companies distinguish hydraulic fracturing as a separate event from well drilling. As a matter of fact, nearly 90 percent of the natural gas wells in the United States have at one time or another used hydraulic fracturing to increase production. However, in terms of the current debate, the term fracking will be used to describe the act of drilling vertically and horizontally and injecting high-pressurized fluids to release and extract oil and natural gas.

The Fracking Process

Fracking begins with geologists—scientists who study rocks and layers of soil to learn about the history of Earth and its life. They determine whether a particular site is likely to produce enough fossil fuel to be worthwhile. Once a site is chosen, it is surveyed and environmental impact studies are completed. Legal rights have to be established. Oil companies need to acquire lease agreements, mineral rights, titles, and right-of-way accesses for the land.

There are many "first steps" to drilling and setting up a fracking operation. "Roughnecks," the colloquial term used for workers on an **oil rig** drilling crew, set up metal drill rigs, some measuring up to 40 feet (12 m) in height. Other equipment includes a slurry blender, fracturing pumps and tanks, and various measuring gauges and controls. Once the drill rig is completed, the roughnecks drill a vertical **borehole** into the

Recycling of water used in fracking is becoming more popular, as water resources are no longer being taken for granted. Here, hoses transfer wastewater from one well to the next.

shale, often a half-mile (0.8 km) or more, depending on the site. Next, the drill is turned at an angle and drilling resumes horizontally, usually one to two miles (1.6 to 3.2 km) across the shale. Engineers carefully measure and monitor the drilling so that the borehole travels through the area containing the greatest amount of trapped oil or natural gas. Once the borehole is complete, it is lined with steel to prevent leakage and **groundwater** contamination.

At this point the actual hydraulic fracturing begins. First, acids are sent down the borehole to clean it. Then a slurry composition, or thick mixture, of water, sand, and chemicals is injected under great pressure into the borehole. The slurry is composed of 90 percent water, 9.5 percent sand, and 0.5 percent chemicals. When the slurry is forced through the

A DEEPER DIVE

Unconventional Fuels

Fracking is most commonly associated with mining for natural gas. However, the technique is also used to extract other "unconventional" fuels, such as shale gas, tight gas, shale oil, and oil from tar sands. The following fuels are also being mined by fracking:

Shale gas: A natural gas trapped in tiny pores of black shale rock.

Tight gas: Natural gas trapped in low-porous silt and sand. These tiny pores are said to be 20,000 times narrower than a human hair.

Sour gas: A natural gas containing significant amounts hydrogen sulfide (H_2S). It is extremely poisonous, corrosive, flammable, and smells like rotten eggs.

Shale Oil: A dense oil containing sulfur and metals such as nickel and vanadium. Shale oil is difficult to pump.

Above ground pumps mechanically lift oil and water out of the wells when there is not enough pressure for the liquid to flow to the surface.

Oil Shale: A type of sedimentary rock that is rich in kerogen (a part of rock that breaks down and releases hydrocarbons when heated). It is both difficult and expensive to process oil shale. An estimated three trillion barrels of this oil exists worldwide.

Tar Sands: Deposits of oil so heavy they do not flow. To extract the oil, enormous amounts of hot liquids are injected into the tar, enough to liquefy the oil so that it can be pumped out.

borehole, the rock bursts open. The sand is forced into the tiny pores in the rock and keeps the pores propped open, allowing the gas to be released. The chemicals then aid in bringing the gas back up through the borehole. Once the flow is consistent, the pressure is released, allowing the slurry to return to the surface to be removed. Sometimes the shale must be fractured many times, and each time requires more water. Some wells have used more than 10 million gallons (38 million L) of water to create greater productivity.

Once the well is producing, the wastewater is recycled, repurposed (such as being used to melt snow and ice on roadways), or transported away. Oil companies are placing an important focus of their research on various means of using less freshwater in the process, and instead using recycled water or seawater. *Bloomberg News* reports that oil companies are aiming to use 25 percent less freshwater in 2014 and beyond.

Increased Output

The Energy Information Agency (EIA) predicts that U.S. natural gas production will have increased 44 percent between the years 2011 and 2040. Almost all this growth will be due to shale gas. In 2006, shale gas production was at three billion cubic feet (85 million cubic meters) per day, and accounted for 5 percent of all natural gas extraction. By 2010, production grew to thirteen billion cubic feet (368 million cubic meters) per day. In 2012, shale gas accounted for 39 percent of all natural gas production in the United States. The *Wall Street Journal* reports that in 2012, production increased at the fastest pace in U.S. history due to fracking. The newspaper quoted Andy Lipow, an oil industry consultant in

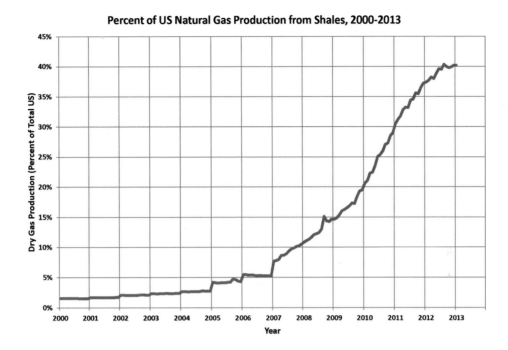

Percent of US Natural Gas Production from Shales, 2000-2013

Houston, as having said, "I don't think anyone expected the magnitude of the change in just one year. It's extraordinary." The EIA reports that there are more than 750 trillion cubic feet (21.2 trillion cubic meters) of shale gas and twenty-four billion barrels of shale oil already located. In the past, these resources would have gone undeveloped, but recent technology— horizontal drilling and high-pressure fluid injection—are providing the key to extracting these much-needed resources.

Demand

Presently, 25 percent of the energy used in the United States comes from burning natural gas. It is used in nearly half of all U.S. homes for heating, cooling, and cooking. It also is the fuel source for one-fourth of

A DEEPER DIVE

Shale Plays

Sites where oil companies are actively looking for and producing shale oil and gas are called **shale plays**. Shale plays are located throughout the country, including:

- Woodford shale natural gas fields in Oklahoma. Wells are 6,000 to 12,000 feet (1,829 to 3,658 m) deep.

- The Bakken spans North Dakota, South Dakota, Montana, and the Canadian province of Saskatchewan, in what is called the Williston Basin. It is believed that the play contains ten to twelve billion barrels of oil and two trillion cubic feet (57 million cubic meters) of natural gas.

- Eagle Ford spans Southwest Texas to East Texas and measures about 400 miles (644 km) long. The shale contains oil, liquid natural gas, and dry gas, or methane.

- Granite Wash is located in the panhandles of Texas and Oklahoma. Layers of trapped oil and gas are 11,000 to 15,000 feet (3,353 to 4,572 m) deep at the site of a prehistoric stream.

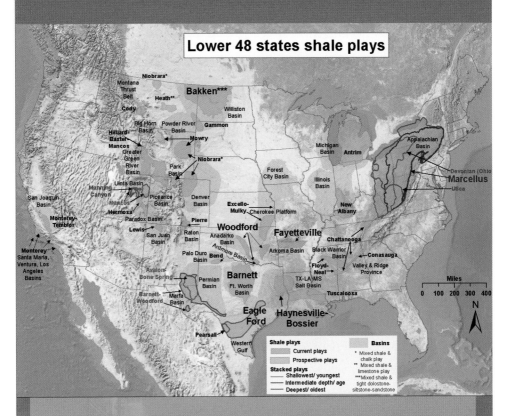

Lower 48 states shale plays

- Haynesville is one of the most productive shale plays, producing 6.2 billion cubic feet (176,000 cubic meters) of natural gas daily.

- Marcellus is a 95,000-square-mile (246,048-square-kilometer) shale bed under Pennsylvania, New York, Maryland, West Virginia, and eastern Ohio. It is the second largest gas shale deposit in the world, and believed to be the largest in the United States. It is believed the Marcellus holds 500 trillion cubic feet (14.2 trillion cubic meters) of natural gas. Most of the wells are in Pennsylvania.

- The Utica shale is located underneath the Marcellus shale. It is estimated to hold up to 5.5 billion barrels of oil and fifteen trillion cubic feet (425 million cubic meters) of natural gas.

- The Niobrara formation is located in the area of the Rocky Mountains that spans Colorado, Wyoming, Kansas, and Nebraska. Most activity today, however, is in the northeastern corner of Colorado.

- Permian is located in West Texas and New Mexico. It is 250 miles (402 km) wide and 300 miles (483 km) long. It potentially holds 500 million barrels of unconventional fuels and five trillion cubic feet (142 million cubic meters) of natural gas.

- The Barnett Shale is located in North Texas. It is estimated to contain as much as twenty-six trillion cubic feet (736 million cubic meters) of natural gas.

- Monterrey shale field lies beneath 1,750 square miles (4,532 square kilometers) of fertile California farmland. It is thought to hold nearly four times the amount of shale oil than the Bakken shale. The Monterrey shale field contains an estimated 15.4 billion barrels of crude oil.

Other shale plays are found in Louisiana, Arkansas, Tennessee, Mississippi, Utah, and North Carolina.

the nation's electric power needs. Since 2010, approximately 30 percent of natural gas was used for electric power generation, 30 percent for manufacturing and industry, 20 percent for heating homes and businesses, and 20 percent for other commercial uses. Industries in which natural gas is primarily consumed include pulp and paper, metals, chemicals, petroleum refining, clay and glass, and food processing. It is used in small quantities (about 1 percent) in vehicles, generally public buses and some commercial truck fleets.

Pure natural gas is clean-burning methane gas. An important use for methane is making a **synthesis gas** called methyl alcohol, which is processed by mixing methane with oxygen and water. Methyl alcohol has a wide variety of applications, including making perfumes, dyes, formaldehyde, and **acetic acid**. It is also mixed with diesel to form biodiesel, and serves as an additive to gasoline to make cleaner burning gasoline.

Methane gas also has a major use in agriculture: It is mixed with nitrogen from the atmosphere to make a chemically stable fertilizer. Oil prices soared in the 2000s, and the cost of producing fertilizer in the United States was the highest in the world. This forced U.S. farmers to import fertilizer from other countries. Since 2009, however, natural gas production in the United States has expanded. As a result, fuel costs have lowered, and U.S. fertilizer manufactures can thereby produce their product less expensively.

A DEEPER DIVE

Kyoto Protocol

The Kyoto Protocol to the United Nations Framework Convention on Climate Change was drafted in Kyoto, Japan, in 1997. The Protocol is an international agreement that legally binds countries to reduce emissions of carbon dioxide (CO_2) and other greenhouse gases. Each country is asked to set a target limit of greenhouse gases that they expect to release into the atmosphere. The convention took into account that developed countries are more responsible for the high levels of greenhouse gases due to 150 years of industrial emissions. Thus, the Protocol made greater demands on developed nations using the principal of "common but differentiated responsibilities." This means that while all countries share responsibility for their greenhouse gas emissions, countries with more wealth and greater technology are expected to make larger reductions. The United States, the largest emitter of greenhouse gases,

One hundred thirty-four countries convened in Poland in November 2013 to discuss reduction of carbon emissions with a goal of limiting the global increase of temperature to just 2 degrees Celsius (3.6 degrees Fahrenheit).

was assigned a reduction of CO_2 emissions by 5.2 percent by 2012.

The United States signed the first draft of the Protocol in 1998, but never ratified it, or made it into law. There are 192 countries that did sign and ratify the Protocol. A new commission is scheduled to meet in Paris in 2015 to make amendments.

The Pros and Cons of Natural Gas and Fracking

Energy Spending

Proponents, meaning those in favor, of fracking point out that this new method of producing fossil fuels contributes to lower energy costs, more jobs, energy independence, and a reduction of **greenhouse gases**. Merrill Matthews of the Institute for Policy Innovation, says, "Fracking has dramatically increased the supply of natural gas, which has, one, turned the United States into one of the top producers—if not the top producer—of natural gas in the world, and, two, reduced costs so much that natural gas has become cheap."

Individual citizens and governments alike benefit from the recovery of natural gas and shale oils. Industry economists from the American Petroleum Institute predict that 600,000 new jobs related to the industry will be created by 2030. American manufacturing and chemical industries are enjoying the benefits of lower costs for energy. The American Chemistry Council reported that a 25 percent increase in ethane (a byproduct of natural gas) had become available to use in manufacturing. Lower operating costs for manufacturers could add more than 400,000 jobs across all sectors, or areas, of the economy and provide more than $4 billion in state and federal taxes. The council's report also cited the added ability to have access to more chemicals at lower costs, which makes the U.S. chemical industry more competitive globally. The National Association of Manufacturers estimated that increased shale gas production will lower natural gas prices and help the nation's manufacturers employ thousands of new workers.

Welders constructing a natural gas pipeline must be highly skilled and ready for any emergency.

A DEEPER DIVE

Going Places

Once out of the ground, the natural gas is processed to remove **impurities**, or unwanted substances that prevent it from being pure. This process sometimes takes place at the well site, other times in a gas processing plant. After processing, the natural gas is usually transported by pipelines assisted by pumping stations throughout the system. Sometimes, natural gas is chilled to -260 degrees Fahrenheit (-162 Celsius) to change it into a liquid called "liquefied natural gas" (LNG), which can be stored in tanks and transported by truck, train, or ship. The demand for natural gas goes beyond fuel, however.

As exports of U.S. liquid natural gas increase, U.S. ports will see more LNG container ships such as this one. LNG exports will create more jobs in the construction, shipbuilding, transportation, and maritime industries.

In 2010, the federal government collected $9.7 billion in royalties and leases, as well as $8.5 billion paid by oil companies in federal income taxes. As production increases, so do these payments. Bruce McKenzie Everett, professor of International Business at Tufts University, notes, "Fracking creates jobs, but that's not the most important way to measure its economic effect. The cost of everything we purchase has an energy component to it, either in its manufacture or its shipping or its packaging. So it is very important to the economy to have energy prices that are relatively low."

Environment and Savings

Due to lower costs and greater availability, the increased use of natural gas in home heating, manufacturing, and electricity generation in lieu of oil and coal has led to reduced carbon dioxide (CO_2) emissions. In 2012, the United States' CO_2 emissions fell 5.2 percent to 5,293 million metric tons—a 291-million-metric-ton decrease from 1997. Proponents of fracking point out that of all the developed countries that signed the Kyoto Protocol, the United States—which never even ratified the Protocol—is the only country that reached its target of a 5 percent reduction in CO_2 emissions. Merrill Matthews of the Institute for Policy Innovation attributes this reduction to the greater use of natural gas. He warns, "Limiting fracking, which would reduce U.S. natural gas production, would likely have the effect of increasing CO_2 emissions."

Bloomberg News encourages the continued use of fracking for natural gas extraction, stating that fracking creates stable and abundant natural gas supplies that lowers the cost of fuel and can deliver clean, efficient energy for "many generations to come."

CRITICAL THINKING

- Supporters of fracking point out that natural gas will reduce the cost of energy for consumers. Will the cost of cleaning up pollution and other damage done to the environment cancel out the fuel cost savings?

- Fracking has created an oversupply of natural gas. As a result, profits once earned by oil and coal manufacturers have declined. Has this driven oil companies to reduce their production—or should it? Why?

- Should the government become involved in maintaining the current level of fracking oil and gas production? Why or why not? If so, in what ways?

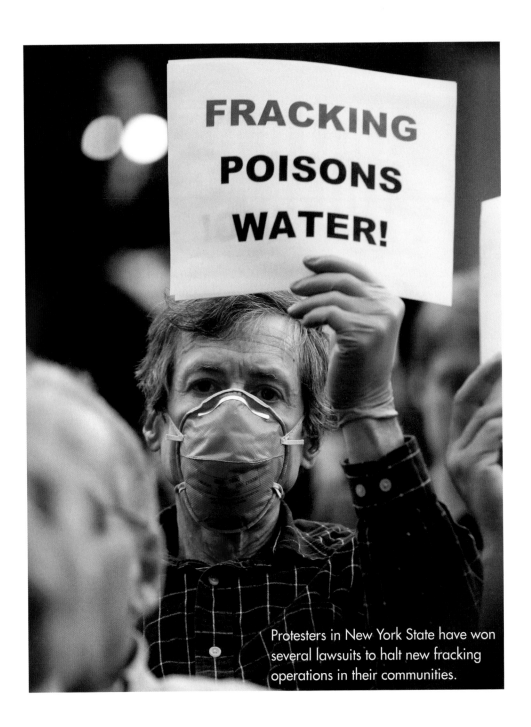

Protesters in New York State have won several lawsuits to halt new fracking operations in their communities.

Chapter 3

A Challenge to the Environment

Hydraulic fracturing takes a toll on the environment. According to author and journalist Alex Prud'homme, "Hydrofracturing is not a gentle process. Sucking oil and gas from dense shale formations involves drilling, explosions, toxic chemicals, and millions of gallons of water pumped at crushing pressures." He also points out the many variables that contribute to the difficulty and safety of each hydrofracturing operation. For every site, there is a different community, a different geology, and a different climate.

For people in Texas, Wyoming, or Oklahoma, oil and gas drilling and extracting have been a familiar and major part of their economy. For communities in North Dakota, where a new natural gas fracking boom has occurred, some residents are excited about their growing economy, while others are concerned that after the boom, there may be a bust. Colorado and California communities have a strong tradition of environmental action, and many shale plays are located in scenic and environmentally sensitive areas. Residents in the Great Plains communities are often divided. Some see fracking as an important new source of income, while others fear contamination of the large

A methane contamination of a Pennyslvania family's drinking water well was so toxic that the homeowners could light a match and set water from the faucet on fire.

underground **aquifer**—a layer of rock or sand that can absorb and hold water—that supplies water for farms and ranches. In the Northeast, there is much controversy over fracking in the Marcellus Shale. Again, many welcome the new sources of income and jobs, while just as many fear environmental damage. Some oil companies respond to community concerns by holding town hall meetings. They may promise to improve infrastructures such as wastewater treatment facilities and roadways. They may also contribute to communities in other ways, such as donating to schools or parks. But other companies are not as accommodating, and leave behind destroyed roadways and polluted land and water.

Each oil well poses its own distinct challenges. For example, many fracking wells in Texas are only 1,000 to 1,500 feet (304.8 to 457 m) deep, and require much less water and pressure than wells in Oklahoma, where some are as deep as 10,000 feet (3,048 m). Other wells may suffer "leak-off," where fracking fluids do not follow the channels made in the rock. Instead, they leak into surrounding rock, causing loss of fluid and effectiveness. Most oil companies meet those challenges most of the time. However, there have been significant failures during both the drilling and extracting processes that have polluted the air, poisoned the water, and threatened the health and safety of people and livestock. Workers have been injured, and several have been killed in well site explosions. Around the country there are reports of contamination from fracking fluids and escaping methane.

Well Construction

Serious concerns over fracking start with the construction of the well. Oil wells have long dotted many regions of the country. However, horizontal wells in which fracking techniques are employed are substantially larger and more expensive to drill and maintain. The process of constructing fracking wells includes ground clearing, excavating, grading, concrete mixing, backfilling, dumping, blasting, and drilling. The well pad (or drilling platform) tanks, impoundment ponds, and other infrastructure require the use of eight or nine acres (3.2 or 3.6 hectares) of land, according to the Nature Conservancy. Wide swaths, or strips, of

A DEEPER DIVE

"Fraccidents"

Some opponents of fracking have dubbed fracking accidents "fraccidents." There are numerous incidents in which residents have been evacuated and/or threatened by fires, explosions, or contaminated water. Many such accidents have occurred in states lying over the Marcellus Shale. In the small community of Dayton, Pennsylvania, residents were evacuated when a well casing failed and methane entered underground water and traveled for a third of a mile. In Dimock, Pennsylvania, more than 8,000 gallons (30,000 L) of contaminated drilling wastes spilled into nearby water systems. As Christopher Bateman writes in *Vanity Fair*, "Dimock is now known as the place where, over the past two years, people's water started turning brown and making them sick, one woman's water well spontaneously combusted, and horses and pets mysteriously began to lose their hair."

In the rural community of Avella, Pennsylvania, a wastewater impoundment pond exploded and caught fire. It burned for six hours, sending flames 200 feet (61 m) in

Wastewater discharged from a treatment plant entered into this stream, affecting the health of native fish, wildlife, and vegetation.

the air, and spewed thick black smoke visible from miles away. In later tests at the site, arsenic found in the soil was at 6,000 times the permissible level. In northeastern Pennsylvania's Leroy Township, there was a well casing explosion. *Popular Mechanics* magazine described the catastrophe as having been "a double dose of bad luck: mechanical failure coupled with bad weather." After a period of steady rains, the well casing cracked open and leaked tens of thousands of gallons of contaminated water into the impoundment pond, which was already full due to rains. The toxic waste spilled out, poisoning the surrounding environment.

Opponents have many concerns about fracking, and feel there are too many unanswered and unanswerable questions regarding its effect on health, safety, and environmental protection.

Citizens living and working near natural gas pipelines live with the daily risk of accidents, spills, and explosions.

land must be cleared for the well pad. Blasting and clearing for new roads to access the fracking site, as well as its adjunct facilities construction offices, storage facilities, and pumping stations is required. Heavy truck traffic and new pipelines add to the impact felt by nearby communities.

Air and Noise Pollution

Well drilling and well site maintenance contribute considerably to air and noise pollution. Heavy construction equipment releases noxious, or harmful, fossil fuel vehicle emissions as well as diesel-powered generator emissions. An average fracking construction site can use from 900 to 1,300 truckloads of materials. Blasting activities release carbon monoxide, nitrogen oxides, and particulates into the air, as well as dust that can lead to dust pneumonia in livestock and wildlife. In 2013, the National Institute for Occupational Safety and Health (NIOSH) tested possible fracking sites for silica, a mineral found in rock and sand and a known cause of lung disease. Levels were found that dangerously exceeded the allowable amount as established in NIOSH regulations. During windless periods, odors are a nuisance to nearby residents. Methane, the chief component of natural gas, contributes twenty times more to climate change than carbon dioxide over a 100-year span. Impoundment storage ponds hold wastewater, which evaporates and releases toxic chemicals such as benzene and xylene into the air. Gases released during fracking contribute to the creation of **smog**, or fog made heavier and darker by smoke and chemical fumes. Lisa Jackson, a former head of the Environmental Protection Agency (EPA), confirmed that in rural areas where wells are present, "You are going to have huge smog problems where you never had them before. There is a lot of activity around those wells and that has an impact on air quality."

A worker stands above a potentially toxic mixture of fracking chemicals.

Noise during the construction phase is excessive. Bulldozers, heavy construction trucks and earthmovers, drilling rigs, blasting equipment, and diesel

A DEEPER DIVE

Going to Bat Against Fracking

Cooperstown, New York, is the home of the National Baseball Hall of Fame. Sitting on a portion of the Marcellus Shale, the town is also home to a fierce battle over fracking. Beginning in 2011, oil companies have been blasting the area, searching for the best sites to drill, while disturbing the peace and quiet of this famous little town. Along with nearby communities, citizens of Cooperstown formed an anti-fracking group that was joined by the Cooperstown Chamber of Commerce and the National Baseball Hall of Fame. While pro-fracking organizations and some local businesses and landowners who stand to gain from fracking leases actively supported fracking, the anti-fracking groups obtained a temporary fracking ban. Said one member of the anti-fracking group, "The essence of this area is its rural, nineteenth-century landscapes. Industrial shale gas extraction would completely destroy

STATEWIDE BAN ON HYDROFRACKING gasmain.org

FRACK catskillcitizens.org

Drilling isn't safe

YES

NEW Y AGAINST

YES WE CAN BAN FRACKING

Protesters gather outside the New York State capital to demand a ban on fracking due to environmental and economic concerns.

this region's biggest assets." In a town hall meeting, Chip Northup, an oil and gas investor and expert on the industry, responded to questions about fracking in New York State, saying, "I don't think anything's going to happen in the next twenty years."

The infrastructure of small towns and country roads were never designed to accommodate the constant flow of large trucks and heavy machinery traveling to and from fracking sites.

engines contribute to high levels of disruption. The blasting is loud, and in areas near denser populations, the sound exceeds EPA standards. Noise from drilling can be as much as 115 decibels at the source, a level that can cause hearing damage. Drilling noises can cause nonstop, twenty-four-hour aggravation for one to two months or more. Once drilling in an area is completed, noise continues to be an issue because of truck traffic, as well as the heavy equipment used to load and dispose of wastewater.

Water Supply

A major issue in the debate over fracking is its impact on water supplies. Water is the largest component of fracking fluids. Most fracking operations draw water from local water resources. In the initial drilling process alone, fracking wells require 6,000 to 600,000 gallons (22,712 to 2.3 million L) of water. The exact amount depends on the depth and location of the oil and gas, and the type of rock formation present. Few environments can replenish that amount of water easily, especially in dry regions such as Texas, North Dakota, or California. During a well's productive period, as much as four million gallons (1.5 million L) of water will be used. In Texas, the Eagle Ford shale wells have used more than twelve million gallons (15.1 million L) of water. In many regions where fracking occurs, conflict arises over water use. In dry regions, ranchers and farmers, as well as businesses and residents, find themselves competing with oil companies for limited water supplies.

Water Quality

Shale formations containing oil and natural gas are also connected by cracks and channels to groundwater, underground streams, and aquifers. Opponents are concerned that fracking chemicals, methane, and other gases can easily leak and find their way into resources for drinking water. Major oil and gas companies are normally very thorough and responsible during the fracking process, although accidents definitely occur. Independent drillers, or **wildcatters**, have been found to be less cautious. The potential for water contamination is undeniable under any operation. Drills and boreholes can fail, casings can crack and leak, and trucks transporting wastewater and chemicals can be involved in accidents. Storage facilities and impoundment sites can leach—or dissolve out— chemicals into the groundwater or the tanks and ponds that can overflow and pollute nearby streams and rivers. In 2011, a Congressional report

A DEEPER DIVE

Shaking Ground

Researchers at the United States Geologic Survey (USGS) reported that during the three decades leading into 2000, **seismic** events in the middle region of the country, from Ohio to Texas, averaged twenty-one earthquakes each year. The number jumped to fifty in 2009, and 134 in 2011. Researchers believe the earthquake activity was influenced, if not directly caused, by fracking, specifically the wastewater injection wells drilled deep in the ground. Fracking uses high-pressure fluids to break the rock, and the trapped gas can sometimes force the fluids as well as the pressure in unwanted directions. Fracking procedures can also destabilize already-existing geologic fault lines— cracks in the Earth that are prone to earthquake activity. David Hayes, the deputy secretary of the U.S. Department of the Interior, said of the USGS report, "Our scientists cite a series of examples for which an uptick in seismic activity is observed in areas where the disposal of wastewater through deep-well injection increased significantly."

Many blame deep wastewater injection wells for a series of earthquakes in Oklahoma.

While many of the earthquakes reported in recent years have been relatively small, they have occurred in areas unused to seismic activity. The waves of pressure stemming from deep injection wells can radiate underground and produce a stronger earthquake in a more seismically sensitive area. Conversely, deep water injection wells weaken the surrounding area. Waves from earthquakes occurring in distant parts of the world can travel underground and compromise fracking sites. In 2010, a major earthquake in Chile sent shock waves underground that eventually triggered an earthquake in Prague, Oklahoma, sixteen hours later. The 2011 earthquake that caused the deadly tsunami in Japan also triggered an earthquake at a fracking site in Snyder, Texas.

cited more than 650 chemicals used in fracking as containing "known, or possible, human **carcinogens** regulated under the Safe Drinking Water Act."

Wastewater Disposal

There are more than 80,000 fracking wells in operation in the country. That number translates into billions of gallons of wastewater and chemicals introduced into the environment each year. After drilling and fracking, the wastewater, called **flowback**, returns to the surface of the well site. The flowback of chemicals return, as does the naturally occurring underground chemicals jarred loose by the high pressure, such as barium, radium, sulfur, and salts. The flowback is pumped out and into tanks. The oil in the mixture floats on the surface, which is then siphoned off and sold. The remaining mixture must be disposed of. Most operations drill deep injection wells to store the waste. When underground rock formations are too unstable to drill deep injection wells, then the waste is stored in large tanks or impoundment ponds. It can also be transported away by truck, pipeline, or train.

Transporting the waste opens the door to the possibility of traffic accidents or pipeline failure. The transported waste is usually sent to sewage treatment plants, many of which are unable to adequately remove the chemicals, radioactive materials, and salts found in the wastewater. After the sewage treatment facilities process the flowback, it is released into the water supply. Salts contained in the flowback can increase the **salinity** of rivers, streams, and groundwater. This leads to the killing of fish, vegetation, and wildlife, and also damages the quality of drinking water. The EPA has fined treatment plants that processed flowback from three Marcellus Shale operations for releasing millions of pounds of salt into the water supply each month. Large oil companies have been fined by the EPA for violations of the Clean Water Act in relation to wastewater disposal. In 2013, Chesapeake Energy was fined $3.2 million, the largest fine up to that date.

The extreme pressure of fracking operations can jar loose naturally-occurring radioactive elements such as barium, radon, and uranium. Flowback brings these substances to the surface. Some evaporate into the air and are ingested by nearby residents, potentially causing lung cancer. Others work their way into the drinking water and can cause serious health problems for humans and animals.

High Cost of Fracking

Extracting natural gas and unconventional fossil fuels by fracking is expensive. Environmental damage notwithstanding, the process itself is not economically sound unless world oil prices are high, reports the Sierra Club, one of the oldest, largest, and most influential grassroots environmental organizations in the United States. The organization explains that fracking, and the accompanying transportation and infrastructure costs involved, are more expensive than typical fossil fuel extraction.

Oil prices and natural gas fracking operations have a boom and bust economic cycle. When world oil prices rise, domestic natural gas production increases. With the abundance of natural gas then available, natural gas prices drop. To compete, world oil prices also drop. With lower oil prices, natural gas is no longer the less expensive fuel.

Communities where there are nearby fracking operations experience heavy costs. Although some landowners receive royalties through leases on their land, the value of their property has decreased as a result of being near fracking sites. Kris Wise, a Texas realtor, said, "The true loss is far greater, and nobody wants to buy homes near gas wells." A number of banks in New York State have refused to make mortgage loans on homes holding gas leases, believing that the homeowners will not be able to resell their homes if there is a gas well on the property. Some insurance companies will not cover property damaged by fracking.

A report by the New York State Department of Transportation calls fracking "ominous," and estimates that the cost of repairing hundreds of miles of roads and bridges to be at least $378 million. In July 2012, Fort Worth, Texas, newspaper the *Star-Telegram* reported that drilling has caused an estimated $2 billion in damages to Texas roads. State and local governments must also bear the heavy cost of cleaning contaminated wells and water supplies.

Local health care resources are also challenged by the increase in illnesses and injuries related to fracking operations, such as chemical spills, fires, and drilling rig accidents. Many of the smaller towns lack the facilities and personnel necessary to treat serious industrial injuries and illnesses related to toxic contaminants.

Fracking does not always provide an influx of income to a community, according to Penn State University professor of agricultural economics Timothy Kelsey. He notes that rental costs in many Pennsylvania fracking towns have tripled. And fracking, he points out, does not spur much local job creation. The best paying fracking jobs are performed by out-of-towners with specialized skills who often send most of their paychecks back to their home state. This does not help the local economies.

CRITICAL THINKING

- When an oil or gas play is determined to be productive, to what extent should governments and communities have input or control on the decision to drill?

- As you have read, communities have undergone serious financial impacts, such as property devaluation and higher taxes to pay for repair of roadways. What other financial impacts on small communities do you see?

Shown here is Wyoming's Upper Green River Valley, a part of the same ecosystem as Yellowstone and Grand Teton National Parks. It is also the site of the nation's fastest growing natural gas fracking wells.

The Pros and Cons of Natural Gas and Fracking

Chapter 4

The Future of Fracking

Proponents of fracking in the United States argue that the process is a means to energy independence. Natural gas and unconventional oils from shale will carry the weight of the nation's energy needs while new and alternative energy sources are developed and improved. Fracking supporters believe that fracking delivers clean and low-cost domestic fossil fuels to the energy consumer. Opponents of fracking say otherwise. They argue that fracking is "a disaster waiting to happen." Elements of the environment—clean water, natural habitats, cities and towns, as well as humans, wildlife, and livestock—are being unnecessarily exposed to serious safety and health risks.

Rules and Regulations

The government estimates that energy demands are presently at twenty million barrels of oil per day. The government is working steadily toward energy independence and natural gas is an important source of domestic fuel. However, everyone must seriously consider environmental concerns. It is rapidly coming to the attention of local, state, and federal

A DEEPER DIVE

A Case in Point

The complexities of whether "to frack or not to frack" are evident in the example of the shale plays of the Green River Formation in Wyoming, Utah, and Colorado. It is considered the largest shale oil deposit in the country, holding one to two trillion barrels of oil. The U.S. Government Accountability Office (GAO) estimated that just half of the potential oil that could be extracted from the region would be "equal to the entire world's proven oil reserves." Supporters say that if just 800 billion barrels of oil from the Green River Formation were extracted, that would be enough fuel to meet energy needs for more than 400 years.

Opponents argue that the cost of drilling and fracking for the oil far exceeds the price at which the oil could be sold. The environment of the Green River Formation is delicately balanced. The project requires so much water that the city of Denver, Colorado, and its vast surrounding farms and ranches could suffer severe water shortages. The potential for environmental accidents is also great.

In the arid west, livestock and crops compete with oil and gas companies for scarce water resources.

Leaks or explosions could damage or pollute underground streams and contaminate drinking water supplies. Fish, wildlife, and native vegetation would also be at risk. The region is relatively arid, so fracking and drilling would create major sandstorms of air pollutants.

governments that greater regulation and oversight of fracking practices will help both sides of the debate reach an acceptable compromise.

Besides the concerns over water quality and environmental protection, a major issue that may cause disagreement is requiring the oil and gas companies to reveal chemicals they use during the fracking process. There are laws in place in eighteen states requiring companies to do so. However, many companies take advantage of what is called the "Halliburton Loophole." This allows oil and gas drillers to keep some of their chemicals secret in order to better compete with one another. FracFocus.org is a publically accessed national database where fracking companies are asked to list their chemicals used. Fearing competition, however, the oil and gas companies are not happy to comply. The state of Texas passed the nation's first regulations requiring disclosure of fracking chemicals. However, more than ten thousand entries out of twelve thousand fracking sites were listed as "secret," "proprietary," or "confidential." The director of Environment Texas reacted by saying, "If the companies argue that fracking is safe, then why are they hiding behind these trade secret loopholes? If you're going to the doctor, you want to know what you have been exposed to."

The International Energy Agency has encouraged oil companies to explain more of their processes and list more of their chemicals to pacify their detractors. The agency suggests that oil companies and environmentalists could begin to have better dialogue if the oil companies adapted and changed some of their practices. The agency has made several recommendations to oil companies, including that they (1) reveal the chemicals being used, (2) become more involved with the communities they enter, (3) monitor water quality, (4) regularly inspect equipment,

Former Secretary of the Interior Ken Salazar calls for government to become more involved in regulating the development of natural gas in a more safe and responsible manner.

(5) improve operating procedures for emergencies and spills, (6) manage water supplies more carefully, (7) clean up and take responsibility for repairs after road construction, (8) accept liability for any water pollution, and (9) reduce air pollution and methane emissions.

The state of Colorado recently passed fracking laws designed to regulate and oversee water quality. These laws require well owners to test and retest water wells before and after drilling. In California, citizens are concerned about new drilling projects in the Monterrey Formation. In January 2014, California passed legislation regarding fracking. State Senator Fran Pavely described the law by saying, "Oil companies will not be allowed to frack in California unless they test the groundwater, notify neighbors, and list each and every chemical on the Internet. This is a first step toward greater transparency, accountability, and protection of the public and the environment." The Illinois Senate voted 52–3 to pass new laws on fracking.

A DEEPER DIVE

The Center for Sustainable Shale Development

Environmentalists and the energy industry have established the Center for Sustainable Shale Development, a new organization in Pittsburgh, Pennsylvania.

The center's mission is to develop standards and guidelines for the fracking industry in the Appalachian area.

Oil and gas companies are encouraged to follow these guidelines. By doing so, the permitting and regulatory process becomes more easily accomplished. Supporters of fracking hope that, by following new and stricter regulations, the public will become more open to the fracking process. The center's environmentalists recognize that hundreds of billions of dollars of shale oil and gas are going to be extracted regardless of any opposition. The environmentalists say that by working with industry experts, fracking will be safer and healthier for all concerned. The center hopes that their efforts will assist other regions in developing similar working relationships.

The following are some of the standards that have been drafted by the center.

Air and Climate Performance Standards

- Limitations on **Flaring**
- Use of **Green Completions**
- Reduced Engine Emissions
- Emissions Controls on Storage Tanks

Surface and Ground Water Performance Standards

- Maximizing Water Recycling
- Development of Groundwater Protection Plan
- Well Casing Design
- Groundwater Monitoring
- Wastewater Disposal
- Impoundment Integrity
- Reduced Toxicity Fracturing Fluid

New efforts are being made by regulators and oil companies to end flaring, or the burning off of methane gas that escapes from wells, and instead capture the natural gas to use for fuel.

Said Illinois governor Pat Quinn, "These are tough regulations that are going to protect and preserve our most valuable resources in our state. We are going to increase home produced energy in our state in one of the most environmentally friendly ways possible."

The EPA is preparing an extensive study of the impact of fracking on the environment, and is beginning to create regulations for the industry. Citing the EPA's Clean Air Act, the EPA has established regulations requiring green completions. A green completion is the process of capturing any escaping natural gas at the wellhead, rather than flaring (burning it off), or allowing it to be released into the atmosphere.

Calling a Truce

People on each side of the fracking debate are recognizing that fracking will not end, and that oil companies will not be allowed to operate without regulations. Scientists are being asked to investigate and produce data that will allow the cleanest and safest ways to extract trapped shale oil and gas. Oil and gas companies are making more effort to cooperate with environmental organizations, and vice versa. Henry Henderson, director of the Natural Resource Defense Council, appreciates the efforts that both sides have made to participate in making decisions that will satisfy all parties concerned. He sees progress in the way some states are beginning to address fracking regulations by including industry representatives and environmental groups. "We have gotten over the frustrating chasm of 'Are you for the environment or for the economy?'" said Henderson. "That is an empty staring contest."

At a wastewater treatment plant, a worker releases the valve of a tanker truck and empties water contaminated by chemicals, salts, and radioactive material from a fracking operation.

What's Next?

Fracking is still a relatively new industry. New methods, procedures, and technologies are being rapidly developed to minimize the impact on the environment. Coiled tubing is one such example. This tubing replaces rigid pipes that must be joined together with a single, long, flexible coiled pipe. The coiled pipe makes it easier, faster, and less expensive to drill. From an environmental perspective, it allows for a smaller drilling footprint and uses fewer fluids.

Oil companies are embracing new technologies designed to make drilling more efficient and precise. They are also developing strategies to recycle wastewater. The goal of several companies is to reuse 90 percent of their wastewater. Using computer monitoring and specialized processes, some companies are approaching that goal. With most of the chemicals removed, the water, though still salty, can be reused in another well rather than being trucked away, stored, or pumped into a deep injection wastewater well.

The price of natural gas continues to decrease as technologies grow more efficient, and consumers have a steady and consistent supply. With the new realization that an enormous amount of fuel stores remain, scientists and creative thinkers are seeking new uses for natural gas. Many want to see more coal-fired electric plants be replaced by low-emission natural gas plants. Some scientists, however, want to further develop natural gas fuel cells, which are clean, highly efficient, and can be used in a number of applications, such as heating, lighting, and powering appliances.

Natural gas, though a fossil fuel, has not been used in transportation to any great degree. Fewer than 200,000 vehicles at present use natural gas for fuel. Now that prices and supplies make natural gas more appealing, many companies operating commercial trucks and delivery vehicles are adding natural-gas-burning vehicles to their fleets. Many public buses

run on natural gas, and new passenger cars are also being introduced to the consumer market.

The government is the largest user of natural gas for vehicles. Almost 50 percent of garbage trucks purchased in 2012 use natural gas.

Many believe natural gas–fueled fuel cells are the wave of the future. Companies are developing them to provide electricity to both businesses and consumers.

Natural gas was the subject of a major scientific study at the Massachusetts Institute of Technology (MIT) in 2011. According to the report, natural gas, although vital to the nation's economy, historically has been overlooked. With the introduction of hydrofracking, trapped shale oil and natural gas have provided the nation an energy windfall. While it's not renewable, or entirely a clean energy, natural gas is by far the most efficient, clean, and inexpensive of fossil fuels. Many believe that with the right environmental controls in place, natural gas will become the "bridge fuel" that steers the country away from dependence on foreign oil supplies and into a future where clean renewable energy sources can take over the majority of the nation's energy needs.

According to the MIT report: "Despite its vital importance to the national economy, natural gas has often been overlooked, or at best taken for granted, in the debate about the future of energy in the United States. Over the past two or three years, this has started to change, and natural gas is finding its place at the heart of the energy discussion."

CRITICAL THINKING

- How large or small a role do you think the U.S. federal government should have in regulating hydrofracking? Why?

- Natural gas produces less carbon emissions than other fossil fuels. What advantages and disadvantages do you see in natural gas having a larger role for use in transportation?

Glossary

acetic acid: a type of acid that is the main substance in vinegar and is used to make plastics, drugs, and make-up

aquifer: a rock layer or sequence that contains water and releases it in amounts large enough to be measured

borehole: a hole bored or drilled in the earth

cap-rock: a layer of relatively impervious rock overlying an oil- or gas-bearing rock

carbon: a naturally abundant element that occurs in many inorganic and in all organic compounds

carcinogen: a cancer-causing substance or agent

flaring: the process of burning natural gas at the wellhead

flowback: the fracking fluids that return to the wellhead once the shale has released the oil or gas

fossil fuel: a fuel source, such as oil, coal, and natural gas, made of decomposed prehistoric organic material

geologist: scientist who studies rocks, layers of soil, water, and the structure of the Earth, as well as the ways in which the Earth was formed

green completions: the process of recapturing, and not flaring off, the natural gas that escapes from the wellhead

greenhouse gas: a gas that traps the heat from the sun below Earth's atmosphere

groundwater: water in a saturated zone beneath Earth's surface

hydraulic fracturing: a process during which wells are drilled so that chemicals and liquids can be injected to open shale rock to release trapped fossil fuels

impoundment pond: a man-made depression used to store wastewater from fracking

impurities: unwanted substances found in something else; impurities prevent substances from being pure

injection well: a well drilled deep in the ground to be used for storage of wastewater from fracking

methane: colorless, odorless, flammable gas; the main component of natural gas

oil rig: a structure holding equipment used for well drilling

petroleum: a thick, flammable, dark-colored crude oil occurring in sedimentary rocks

salinity: the amount of salt in a liquid

sedimentary rock: the type of rock formed from minerals and organic matter compressed over time

seismic: relating to or caused by earthquakes or artificially produced earth tremors

shale: a fine-grained sedimentary rock that may contain oil or natural gas shale oil

shale play: a term used by the oil and gas industry to refer to an area targeted for exploration

smog: an unhealthy mixture of atmospheric pollutants and fog

synthesis gas: a mixture of gases made by steam reacting with natural gas, used for creating organic chemicals and as a fuel

wildcatter: an independent oil prospector

Find Out More

Books

Hillstrom, Kevin, ed. *Fracking*. Detroit, MI: Lucent Books, 2013.

Prud'homme, Alex. *Hydrofracking: What Everyone Needs to Know*. New York, NY: Oxford University Press, 2014.

Thompson, Tamara, ed. *Fracking*. Detroit, MI: Greenhaven Press, 2013. (Kindle edition.)

Websites

Natural Gas Supply Organization

www.naturalgas.org

Learn about the natural gas industry, the environment, new technologies, and explore the process of drilling and extracting.

The United States Department of Energy

www.energy.gov

Discover the history of natural gas drilling and take a look into its future. Environmental and economic topics are also covered.

The United States Energy Information Administration

www.eia.gov

Search this website for statistics on fuel consumption, projections of energy use and resources, financial analysis of energy consumption, greenhouse gas data, and international reports.

The United States Geologic Survey

www.energy.usgs.gov/Generalinfo/AbouttheEnergyProgram.aspx

Find out more about the technologies of oil and gas exploration on this website. Explore rock formations and Earth's geology.

Index

About the Author

Ruth Bjorklund is a former librarian, and has written more than thirty books on topics that include wildlife, science, and medicine. She lives on Bainbridge Island, near Seattle, Washington, where she enjoys hiking and the outdoors. Bjorklund has traveled throughout the Western United States and has visited communities located near natural gas drilling sites. In talking with residents, she found opinions ranging from serious environmental concern to an appreciation for new jobs, income from oil and gas leases, and a less expensive energy source. In the future, she believes that many of our questions will be answered.